MW01228549

Sondra's Sage

TIPS

TO INSURE PASTORAL SANITY!

Reverend Dr. Sondra M. Coleman

Dedicated to the loving memory of my parents and grandparents and to all of the great cloud of witnesses who loved and nurtured me.

Acknowledgments

I give a wealth of thanks to my mentors, the late Bishop Richard Thompson and Mrs. Georgia M. Thompson, Bishop and Mrs. Darryl B. Starnes, Sr., the late Bishop James McCoy and Mrs. Shirley McCoy, Bishop and Mrs. Dennis V. Proctor, Bishop and Mrs. Seth O. Lartey, Dr. G. Ray Coleman, and Dr. Albert J. D. Aymer for your excellence in ministry and the impact your mentorship continues to contribute to my own ministry.

I am grateful to each church I have been privileged to pastor, the Birmingham District, and all the persons within who helped me to develop my leadership and strengthen my love for God.

I can never repay Janice Wilson, Dr. Merchuria Chase Williams, Dr. Mary Love, and Sharon Coleman who assisted me with the labor of editing whether it was years ago with the original TIPS or recently with the revised version.

Thanks seem inadequate for LaKesha Womack, who wears multiple hats in my world but specifically for publishing this work and all that it requires every step of the way.

I could do nothing without the unconditional love of my family and friends who constantly support and pray for me. May God richly bless each of you.

Foreword

On December 11, 1994, I stood to preach my trial sermon at Metropolitan A.M.E. Zion Church. I resigned from corporate America and entered seminary in 1995, received my first pastoral appointment in 1996, and the rest is history.

My years in ministry have proven to be the hardest work I have ever done in my life, but also the most rewarding. This trip down pastoral ministry lane is the most significant journey I have ever taken. Being chosen by God to lead others to Christ is an awesome privilege. My life and ministry has been graced abundantly.

Some of the graces have been disguised. As I walked through the valley of the shadow of death — the death of loved ones, the death of dreams unfulfilled, I learned how to balance the pain with the joy of servanthood in the land of the living. A vital lesson I have learned is that it is absolutely crucial to take time to rest and refresh every now and then.

This work comes out of my sabbatical experience in October 2004 officially lasted for four weeks. Some colleagues expressed surprise and concern that I would be away from the pulpit for a month. But I believe and know that a church with proper leadership should function well--*especially* when the pastor is away.

I returned to the pulpit one month later in November but inwardly, privately, I remained in Sabbath mode. It was the only way for me to continue the reflection I had begun and to discover what I needed to do to permanently keep the tremendous sense of peace I discovered.

A requirement of the fully funded sabbatical was to submit a reflective writing of your time of Sabbath. *Sondra's Sage*: *TIPS to Insure Pastoral Sanity*, was born out of my observations and lessons learned from eight years of pastoral ministry. Today, having experienced twenty years in ministry, I am encouraged to share the TIPS with the larger community. While originally written for pastors, the tips can apply to all leaders (clergy or laity). As we strive to be better each day, may we always remember the goodness of God's grace!

Walking

with

God

Give God your mind, heart and soul and control of your life each day. You can do nothing without God.

• •

Respect other faiths and the right of others to worship differently.

• •

Be grounded in your own theology so that you can defend your beliefs and persuade others to come into the Kingdom.

• •

Feed your spirit. Starve your flesh.

. . . .

Make time for God and develop an authentic relationship with the God of whom you preach.

. . . .

Invest in the wealth of prayer.

. . . .

Be careful of needless distractions.

. . . .

Be sure of your calling and prepare yourself.

•••••••••••••••••••••••••••••

Never feel the need to defend your calling or offend someone who does not believe in its authenticity. That's God's business.

•••••••••••••••••••••••••••••

Be free enough to give up certain liberties for Christ's sake.

•••••••••••••••••••••••••••••

Remember that your priority is prayer and proclamation of the Word.

•••••••••••••••••••••••••••••

Beware of mindless activities and chatter. This can kill you and the church.

•••••••••••••••••••••••••••••

Be inclusive. God is.

•••••••••••••••••••••••••••••

Be bold and courageous. You're walking with God.

•••••••••••••••••••••••••••••

Take risks. You are working for God.

• •

Mind your own business.

• •

When all else fails, remember God never has and never will.

• •

Integrity

Resist the urge to resolve every problem immediately. Learn its history and seek God's guidance before you take any action.

• •

When the tendency to judge comes upon you, look in the mirror.

• •

Practice and live what you preach.

• •

Resist the temptation to allow others to put you on a pedestal. If you get on it, you WILL fall down.

....

Never betray a confidence.

....

If you receive estimated travel expenses and spend less than the estimated amount, return the unused funds to the church.

....

Never engage in an action or a conversation that will put your ministry or family at risk.

• •

Live within your means.

• •

Always take the high road. Integrity follows you.

• •

Be honest. Lying comes back to haunt you and decreases your credibility tremendously.

Keep your word.

• •

Take responsibility for your mistakes and try not to make the same one twice.

• •

Forgive others who offend you, whether they ask for it or not.

• •

Respect has a reciprocal effect. Give it. Get it back.

• •

Leading

like

Christ

Delegate responsibilities.
Challenge people and
engage them in service.
Clarify your expectations.

• •

Focus on solutions
instead of problems. Trust
the God who always wins
to fight your battles.

• •

People look to their
leaders to exhibit
leadership. Exercise your
faith that God will see you
through all things.

• •

Be creative and unpredictable.

• •

Resist the urge to imitate others. Do you.

• •

No guilt trips. Don't give them. Don't take them.

• •

Everyone will not like you. You will not like everyone. Love them anyway.

• •

Be slow to copy exactly what other churches do. What works for one church may not work for yours. Learn the culture of your church.

•••••••••••••••••••••••••••••

Reach for excellence and teach others to do the same. God abhors mediocrity.

•••••••••••••••••••••••••••••

Be flexible. Be not confined by your own mind.

•••••••••••••••••••••••••••••

There is more than one way to do the same thing. Your way may or may not be the best. If it achieves the same goal, allow someone else's way to be utilized.

• •

Be a team player and promote the concepts of collaboration and cooperation.

• •

Never publicly demean the work of a predecessor. The day is coming when someone will follow you.

*What goes around really
does come around.*

• •

*Do not try to fill your
predecessor's shoes.
Wear your own well.*

• •

*Prepare for every
presentation no matter
how smart you are.*

• •

*If there is a need for
change, start with
yourself.*

Lead in the spirit of the law and not the letter.

•••••••••••••••••••••••••••••

Avoid manipulation — manipulating others or allowing others to manipulate you.

•••••••••••••••••••••••••••••

Pray for those who are irregular in their attendance and irresponsible in their commitments.

•••••••••••••••••••••••••••••

Be brave enough to make changes in personnel or committee chairs when necessary.

••••••••••••••••••••••••••••••

Start on time. Do not punish or disrespect the prompt and faithful.

••••••••••••••••••••••••••••••

Give attention to those who are present.

••••••••••••••••••••••••••••••

Taming the Tongue

Observe more. Listen a lot. Talk less.

•••••••••••••••••••••••••••••

Avoid the Moses syndrome. No name - calling.

•••••••••••••••••••••••••••••

Avoid gossip.

•••••••••••••••••••••••••••••

Do not malign those in authority over you.

•••••••••••••••••••••••••••••

Respond positively to adversity instead of reacting negatively. Take time to ponder and gain insight, then handle accordingly.

••••••••••••••••••••••••••••••

Resist the urge to believe everything you hear.

••••••••••••••••••••••••••••••

Apologize when you are wrong and ask for forgiveness.

••••••••••••••••••••••••••••••

Resolve misunderstandings before they become huge problems.

....

Be careful of the questions you ask. There are some things you do not need to know. There are some things you do not want to know.

....

Be not afraid to say, "I don't know."

....

Be not afraid to say "no."

When delivering a eulogy, tell the truth. If the truth about the deceased is not appropriate, just tell the gospel truth.

• •

Be kind. It confuses your enemies.

• •

Smile often. A pleasant look goes a long way.

• •

Have compassion for others. The people you serve need it. You do, too.

Feeding God's People

Do unto the congregation as you would have them do unto you.

• •

Get to know the congregation. Allow them get to know you but guard your personal space.

• •

Always involve the congregation in the work of the church. The church does not live by you alone.

• •

*Do not scold the
congregation from the
pulpit. Preach the Word.*

• •

*Be real before the
congregation. Show them
your heart.*

• •

*Keep your preaching
fresh. Preaching the same
way you always have
makes for a predictable
and possibly dull
preacher.*

• •

Resist the urge to preach the same sermon many times.

• •

Require pre-marital counseling for those considering marriage. It is amazing what couples do not discuss prior to marriage.

• •

Encourage marital counseling. Work hard to keep families together. The stronger the family units in the church, the stronger the church.

Encourage post-marital (divorce) counseling. The aftermath lingers long after the judge's decree.

••••••••••••••••••••••••••••••

Give special attention to children and youth. Never disappoint them. If you do, explain, and make amends to them.

••••••••••••••••••••••••••••••

Resist the urge to return the favor when members tell you what you could do better.

••••••••••••••••••••••••••••••

*Make visitation to the sick
and homebound a priority
and engage the members
to help you. People need
to know the church cares.*

• •

*Take God seriously but
not yourself so much.
Relax and take deep
breaths often.*

• •

*Delve deeply into the
Scriptures so that all may
experience the richness of
God's Word.*

• •

Challenge your congregation to think and do.

• •

Be sure the church is actively present in the community. Know your neighbors and do what it takes for your neighbors to know you.

• •

The Gospel is a social justice Gospel. Lead your congregation to be involved in the fight for justice, civil rights of all and experience the joy of helping those who cannot help themselves.

• •

Give generously. Teach and lead the congregation to experience the joy of worship AND giving.

• •

Never have the congregation earnest waiting for those famous two words, "In conclusion."

• •

Engage the congregation in worship. Don't let it be a "Look at Me" show.

•••••••••••••••••••••••••••••••

Self
Care

*When things get rough,
retreat and recharge.*

• •

*Stress and sin have one
thing in common. They
both kill.*

• •

Laugh. It's contagious.

• •

*Seek counsel from a
professional when you
need help. You cannot be
your own counselor. And
you will need help.*

Confession is good for the soul. Denial is not.

••••••••••••••••••••••••••••••

Make time for yourself.

••••••••••••••••••••••••••••••

Make time for your family.

••••••••••••••••••••••••••••••

Guard your privacy. Your personal life should be private and never the topic of public conversation.

••••••••••••••••••••••••••••••

*Broaden your horizons.
Visit a place you have
never been.*

• •

*Read. Continuous
learning and knowledge of
current events is crucial.*

• •

*Cultivate friendships that
provide inspiration and
support.*

• •

Be a friend, not a lapdog.

• •

*Eat healthily. Exercise
regularly. Rest and repeat.*

•••••••••••••••••••••••••••••

Sondra Coleman

Sondra's Sage was birthed at the end of her first sabbatical in 2004. After deep reflection of her pastoral ministry and an oasis of refreshment, she created a list of TIPS that can be used To Insure Pastoral Sanity! After twenty years of ministry, she realized that these TIPS are not only relevant for the self-care of pastors but can also be used by laity as reminders of how we should engage with others, care for ourselves, demonstrate leadership and most importantly walk with God.

Dr. Sondra Coleman is a former pastor of 17 years in the African Methodist Episcopal Zion Church. She currently serves as the Presiding Elder of the Birmingham District in the Alabama-Florida Episcopal area, Director of Extensions at Hood Theological Seminary, and Adjunct Professor in Pastoral Theology at Hood's Extension site in Greenville, AL.

62089214R00031

Made in the USA
Columbia, SC
01 July 2019